Smoothie Recipes for Kids

Healthy, Delicious, & Non Dairy

Dexter Poin

This smoothie cookbook belongs to:

Hey kids!

Are you ready to roll up your sleeves, and get started on creating some delicious smoothie recipes?

Great!

But first, before you begin. You need to ask yourself, have you ever seen a Gater wear sunglasses indoors?

You are going to love these smoothies! And your parents are going to love that they are also healthy, and made with natural ingredients!

There are even a few green vegetables in a couple of them!

Don't worry! You won't even taste them inside of these delicious smoothies!

So skim through the ingredients, and choose which ones you want to make first. And make your grocery list of ingredients you will need to begin your first smoothie.

Don't forget to have your parents help you chop, and cut the ingredients as needed!

Check this out!

Alongside each smoothie recipes, we have given you a recipe template, to either create variations of your favorite smoothie. Or create brand new smoothie recipes of your own!

There are plenty of smoothie recipe templates for you to create delicious smoothies of your own for a long time!

Keep this smoothie recipe book as your own personal smoothie cookbook!

Have fun blending, and drinking your smoothies!

Table of Contents

Berry Cherry Smoothie

Ingredients:
- 1 1/2 cup fresh cherries, pitted
- 2 dates, pitted
- 1 cup almond milk
- 1 banana
- Ice

Directions:
1. Add all ingredients into the blender and blend until smooth.
2. Serve & drink up!

Nutritional Value (Amount per Serving):
- Calories 215
- Fat 9 g
- Carbohydrates 17 g
- Protein 2 g

Recipe:

Ingredients:

Directions:

Nutrition Info:

Almond & Chocolate Smoothie

Ingredients:
- 4 tbsp almonds
- 1/2 cup fresh cherries - pitted
- 1/2 cup ice cubes
- 1 cup chocolate almond milk

Directions:
1. Add all ingredients into the blender and blend until smooth.
2. Serve immediately and enjoy your smoothie!

Nutritional Value (Amount per Serving):
- Calories 145
- Fat 4 g
- Carbohydrates 36g
- Protein 2 g

Recipe:

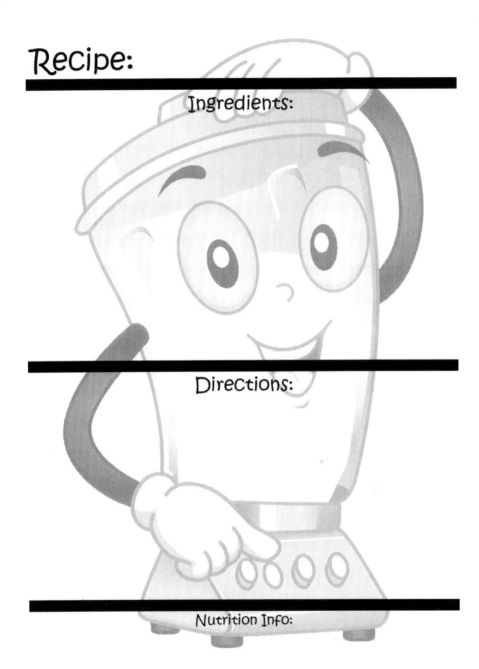

Ingredients:

Directions:

Nutrition Info:

Banana - Anna Smoothie

Ingredients:
- 2 bananas
- 2 cups fresh strawberries
- 1 cup orange juice
- Ice

Directions:
1. Add all ingredients into the blender and blend until smooth.
2. Serve & enjoy your Banana – Anna smoothie!

Nutritional Value (Amount per Serving):
- Calories 207
- Fat 1 g
- Carbohydrates 50 g
- Protein 3 g

Recipe:

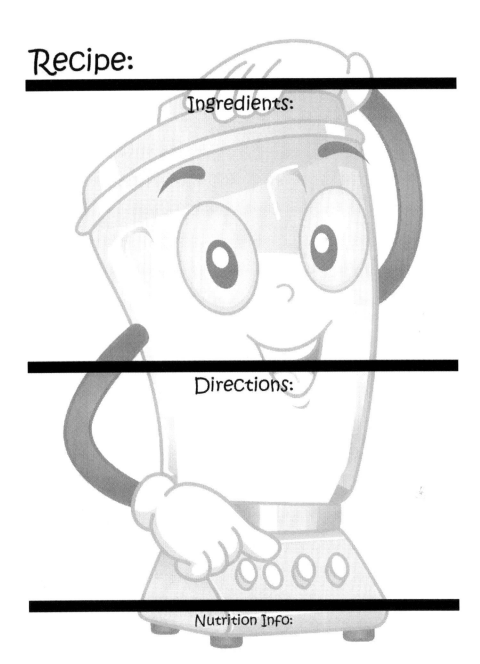

Ingredients:

Directions:

Nutrition Info:

Figaro - Figaro Smoothie

Ingredients:
- 4 fresh figs
- 1 banana
- 1 1/2 cup Chocolate almond milk
- ¼ cup dry oats
- 1 tsp cinnamon
- Ice

Directions:
1. Add all ingredients into the blender and blend until smooth.
2. Serve immediately & drink up!

Nutritional Value (Amount per Serving):
- Calories 331
- Fat 4 g
- Carbohydrates 58 g
- Protein 8 g

Recipe:

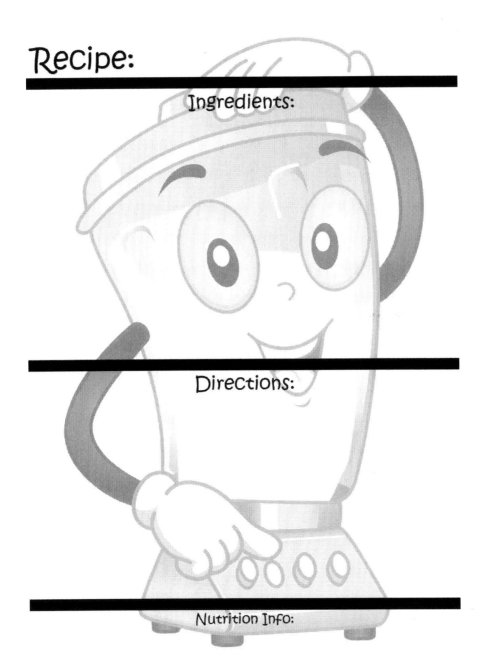

Ingredients:

Directions:

Nutrition Info:

Coo Coo 4 Cantaloupe Smoothie

Ingredients:
- 2 cups Cantaloupe
- 1 cup ice
- 1/2 tbsp Stevia Powder
- 1 cup orange juice
- 8 slices of peaches(1 whole peach)

Directions:
1. Add all ingredients into the blender and blend until smooth.
2. Pour & enjoy your smoothie!

Nutritional Value (Amount per Serving):
- Calories 231
- Fat 1 g
- Carbohydrates 48 g
- Protein 3 g

Recipe:

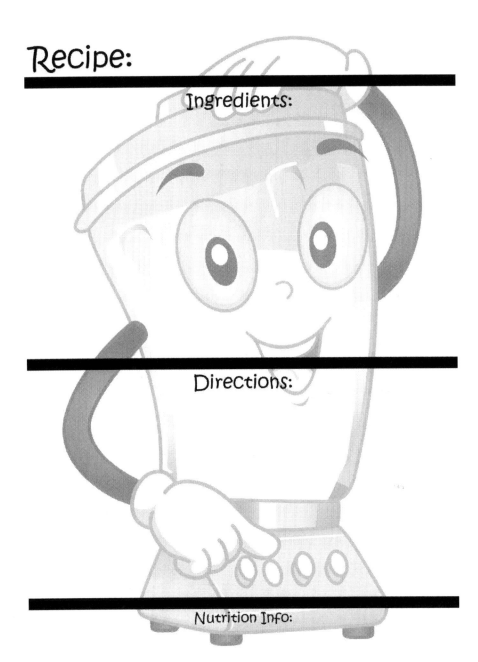

Ingredients:

Directions:

Nutrition Info:

Sweet Green Kiwi Smoothie

Ingredients:
- 1 cup kale, washed(*eat your veggies!*)
- 2 kiwi, peeled and sliced
- 1/2 cup ice cube
- 2 tbsp stevia
- 1 cup plain almond milk
- 1 ripe banana

Directions:
1. Add all ingredients into the blender and blend until smooth.
2. Serve immediately and enjoy! You won't even taste the kale!

Nutritional Value (Amount per Serving):
- Calories 293
- Fat 3 g
- Carbohydrates 64 g
- Protein 7 g

Recipe:

Ingredients:

Directions:

Nutrition Info:

Tango - Mango Smoothie

Ingredients:
- 1 cup mango, diced
- 1 cup plain almond milk
- 1 cup strawberries
- 1 ripe banana
- 2 tangerines

Directions:
1. Add all ingredients into the blender and blend until smooth and creamy.
2. Serve & drink up!

Nutritional Value (Amount per Serving):
- Calories 258
- Fat 2 g
- Carbohydrates 63 g
- Protein 4 g

Recipe:

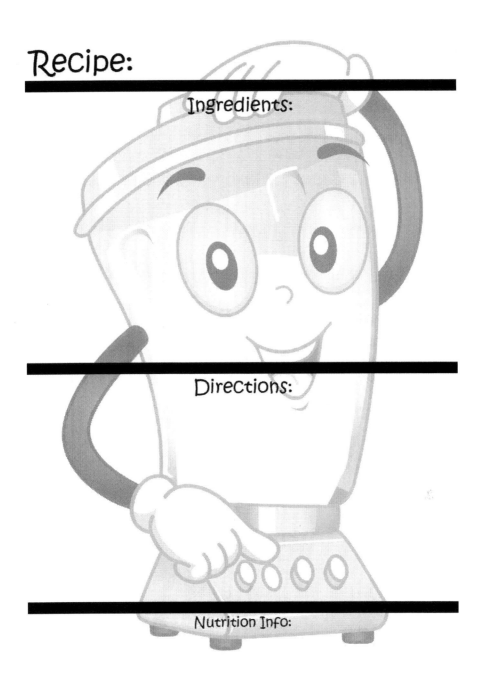

Ingredients:

Directions:

Nutrition Info:

Green Machine Smoothie

Ingredients:
- 2 cups pineapple, cut into chunks
- 1 avocado, remove seed and scoop out
- 1 cup plain almond milk
- 1 large banana
- 2 cups chopped baby spinach (yummy!)
- 1 cup pineapple juice
- Ice

Directions:
1. Add all ingredients into the blender and blend until smooth.
2. Serve & enjoy the sweetness!

Nutritional Value (Amount per Serving):
- Calories 451
- Fat 23 g
- Carbohydrates 79 g
- Protein 4 g

Recipe:

Ingredients:

Directions:

Nutrition Info:

Pineapple Orange Smoothie

Ingredients:
- 1/2 cup pineapple chunks
- ½ cup coconut milk
- 3/4 cup fresh orange juice
- 6 tbsp vanilla non dairy ice cream
- 1 banana

Directions:
1. Add all ingredients into the blender and blend until smooth.
2. Serve & enjoy!

Nutritional Value (Amount per Serving):
- Calories 200
- Fat 2 g
- Carbohydrates 47 g
- Protein 4 g

Recipe:

Ingredients:

Directions:

Nutrition Info:

Bananas Are Born Green Smoothie

Ingredients:
- 1 cup kale, remove stems
- 2 bananas
- 1 cup pineapple juice
- 2 tbsp chia seeds
- 1 lime - juice
- 2 cups pineapple chunks

Directions:
1. Add kale and juice in blender and blend until smooth.
2. Now add remaining ingredients into the blender and blend again until smooth.
3. Serve immediately and enjoy!

Nutritional Value (Amount per Serving):
- Calories 268
- Fat 3 g
- Carbohydrates 62 g
- Protein 3 g

Recipe:

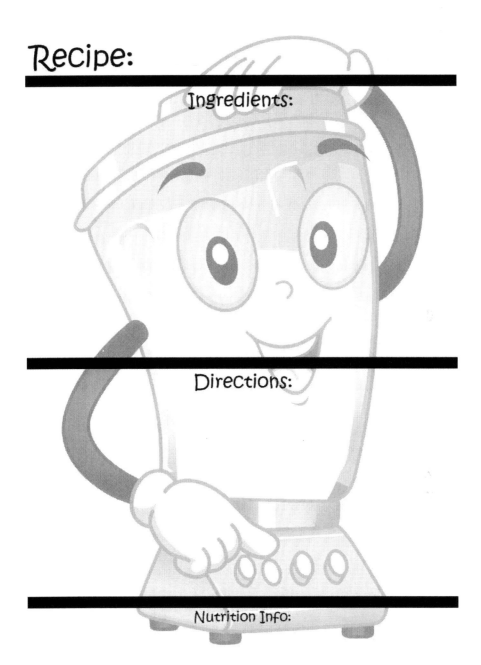

Ingredients:

Directions:

Nutrition Info:

Watermelon Lovers Smoothie

Ingredients:

- 4 cups watermelon chunks!!!!!
- 2 cups strawberry
- 1 inch ginger
- 2 tbsp chia seeds
- 2 whole limes - juice
- Ice
- Sea Salt

Directions:

1. Add all ingredients into the blender except juice from 1 lime, and blend until smooth.
2. Serve with salt and squeezed lime on top! Drink with a straw.

Nutritional Value (Amount per Serving):

- Calories 270
- Fat 1 g
- Carbohydrates 76 g
- Protein 1 g

Recipe:

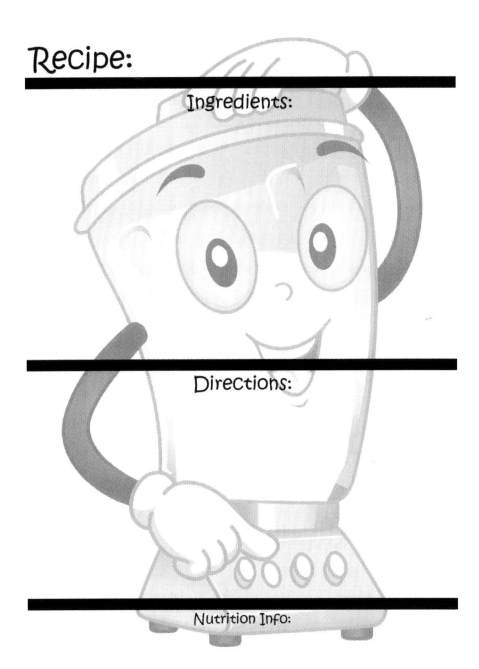

Ingredients:

Directions:

Nutrition Info:

Energy Minty Watermelon Smoothie

Ingredients:
- 1 lime - juice
- 2 cups watermelon chunks
- 3 fresh mint leaves
- 2 cups fresh strawberries
- ice

Directions:
1. Add all ingredients into the blender and blend until smooth.
2. Serve immediately and enjoy!

Nutritional Value (Amount per Serving):
- Calories 252
- Fat 1 g
- Carbohydrates 65 g
- Protein 1 g

Recipe:

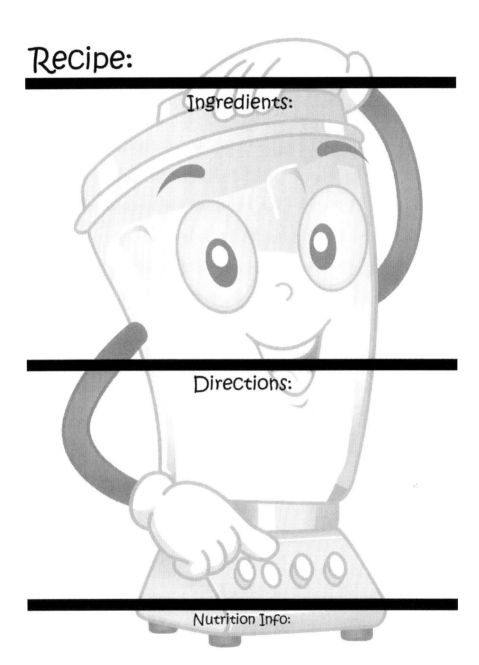

Ingredients:

Directions:

Nutrition Info:

Papaya Smoothie

Ingredients:
- 1 cup papaya chunks
- 1 inch ginger piece
- 3/4 cup vanilla almond milk
- 1 cup ice cubes
- 1 cup pineapple chunks
- 1 lime - juice
- 1 banana

Directions:
1. Add all ingredients into the blender and blend until smooth.
2. Serve immediately and enjoy!

Nutritional Value (Amount per Serving):
- Calories 255
- Fat 1 g
- Carbohydrates 58 g
- Protein 2g

Recipe:

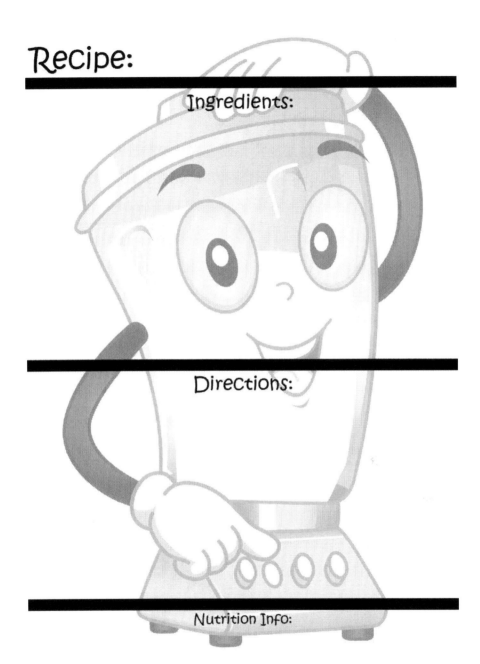

Ingredients:

Directions:

Nutrition Info:

Tropical Fruit Smoothie

Ingredients:
- 1 cup papaya, cubed
- 1 cup vanilla coconut milk
- 1 cup pineapple chunks
- 1/2 tbsp Tropical flavored Stevia
- Ice

Directions:
1. Add all ingredients into the blender and blend until smooth.
2. Serve immediately and enjoy!

Nutritional Value (Amount per Serving):
- Calories 196
- Fat 2 g
- Carbohydrates 44 g
- Protein 3 g

Recipe:

Ingredients:

Directions:

Nutrition Info:

Chocolate Banana Smoothie

Ingredients:
- 2 tsp cocoa powder
- 2 large bananas
- ½ cup blueberries
- 1/2 cup ice cubes
- 2 tsp Stevia
- 1 1/2 cups Chocolate Cashew milk

Directions:
1. Add all ingredients into the blender and blend until smooth and creamy.
2. Serve & enjoy!

Nutritional Value (Amount per Serving):
- Calories 149
- Fat 2 g
- Carbohydrates 63g
- Protein 3 g

Recipe:

Ingredients:

Directions:

Nutrition Info:

Pumpkin Pie Smoothie

Ingredients:
- 1 cup canned pumpkin
- 1 banana
- 1 tsp Ground nutmeg
- 1 tsp pumpkin pie spice
- 1 tsp cinnamon
- 6 ice cubes
- 1 cup vanilla almond milk - or
- 1 cup vanilla non dairy ice cream

Directions:
1. Add all ingredients except nutmeg into the blender and blend until smooth.
2. Garnish with ground nutmeg and serve!

Nutritional Value (Amount per Serving):
- Calories 260
- Fat 3 g
- Carbohydrates 59 g
- Protein 3 g

Recipe:

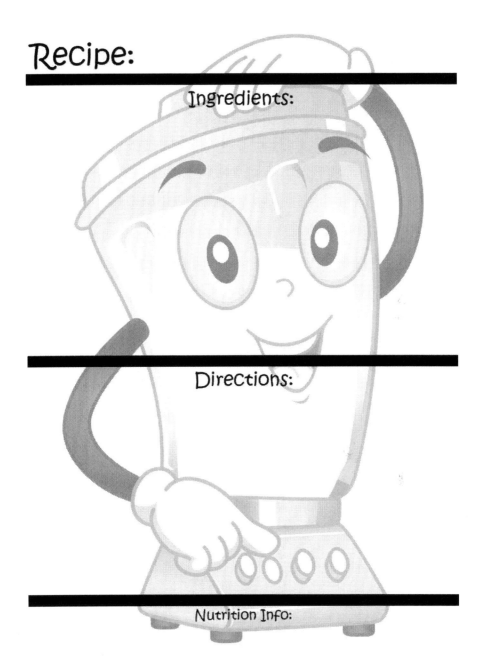

Ingredients:

Directions:

Nutrition Info:

Berry - Berry Smoothie

Ingredients:
- 1 1/2 cup raspberries
- 1 kiwi, peeled and sliced
- 1 cup blueberries
- 1 cups orange juice
- 1 cups strawberries
- Ice

Directions:
1. Add strawberries, blueberries and raspberries in blender and blend until smooth.
2. Then add ice, orange juice, and sliced kiwi, and blend again until smooth.
3. Serve immediately and enjoy!

Nutritional Value (Amount per Serving):
- Calories 266
- Fat 1 g
- Carbohydrates 90 g
- Protein 4 g

Recipe:

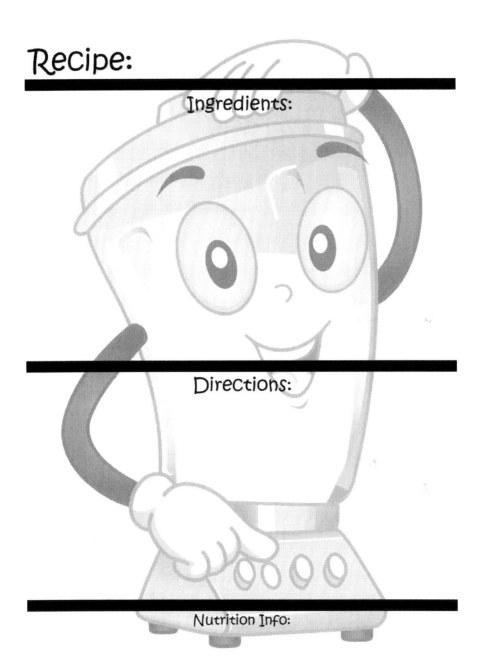

Ingredients:

Directions:

Nutrition Info:

Chunky Booster Smoothie

Ingredients:
- 1/2 cup pineapple chunks
- 1 whole peach sliced
- 1 green apple sliced
- 1 cup strawberries
- 1 1/2 cups orange juice
- 6 ice cubes

Directions:
1. Add all ingredients into the blender and blend until smooth and creamy.
2. Serve, and enjoy!

Nutritional Value (Amount per Serving):
- Calories 251
- Fat 1 g
- Carbohydrates 67 g
- Protein 5 g

Recipe:

Ingredients:

Directions:

Nutrition Info:

Grape- Ape- Fruit Smoothie

Ingredients:
- 1 cup grapefruit juice
- 1 cups fresh raspberries
- 1 whole green apple - sliced
- 1 whole lime - juice
- 2 fresh bananas
- ice

Directions:
1. Add all ingredients into the blender and blend until smooth.
2. Serve & enjoy!

Nutritional Value (Amount per Serving):
- Calories 260
- Fat 1 g
- Carbohydrates 62 g
- Protein 3 g

Recipe:

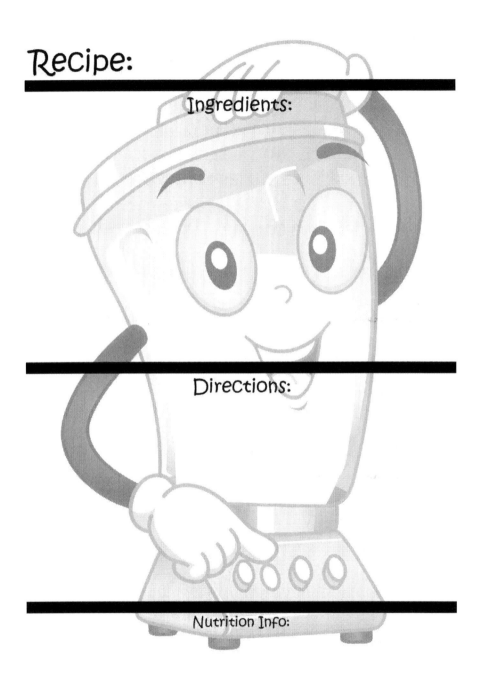

Ingredients:

Directions:

Nutrition Info:

Green Thunder Smoothie

Ingredients:

- 1 cup papaya, cubed
- 1 cup apple juice
- 1 cup pineapple chunks
- 1 cup baby spinach
- 1 banana
- Ice

Directions:

3. Add all ingredients into the blender and blend until smooth.
4. Serve immediately and enjoy!

Nutritional Value (Amount per Serving):

- Calories 306
- Fat 1 g
- Carbohydrates 75 g
- Protein 2 g

These are some great smoothies!

Are you excited to begin creating smoothie recipes of your own?

Awesome!

Here are some more smoothie recipe templates, for creating your very own smoothie cookbook!

Share them with your friends, and family!

When you need more smoothie templates, & recipes, look up Recipe Junkies on Amazon. Plenty of them for you to choose from.

Recipe:

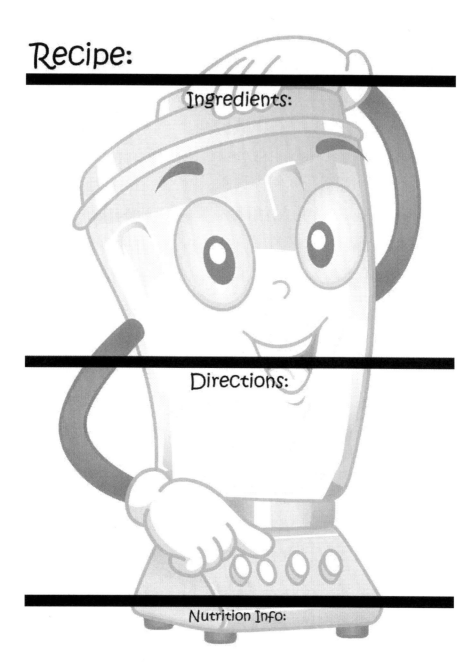

Ingredients:

Directions:

Nutrition Info:

Recipe:

Ingredients:

Directions:

Nutrition Info:

Recipe:

Ingredients:

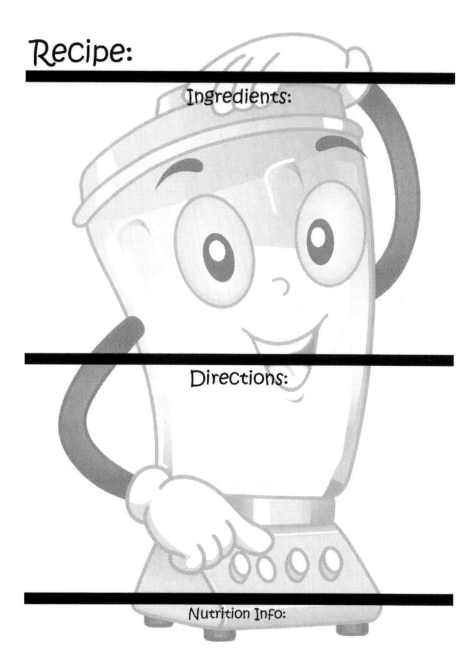

Directions:

Nutrition Info:

Recipe:

Ingredients:

Directions:

Nutrition Info:

Recipe:

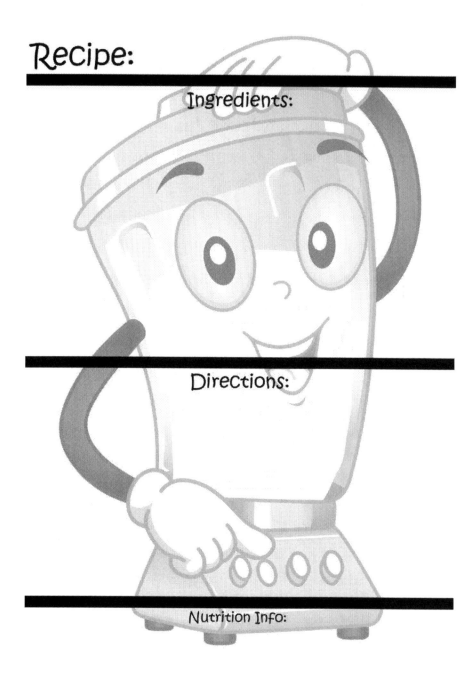

Ingredients:

Directions:

Nutrition Info:

Recipe:

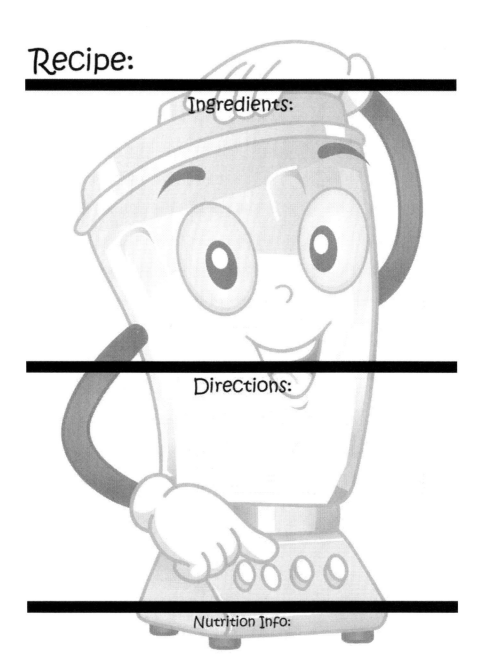

Ingredients:

Directions:

Nutrition Info:

Recipe:

Ingredients:

Directions:

Nutrition Info:

Recipe:

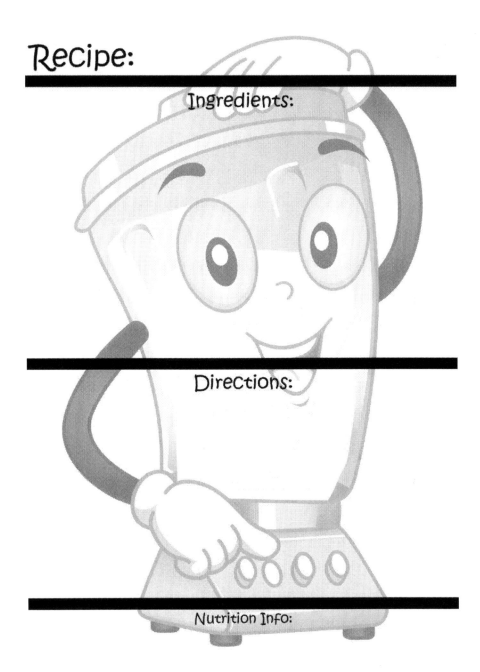

Ingredients:

Directions:

Nutrition Info:

Recipe:

Ingredients:

Directions:

Nutrition Info:

Recipe:

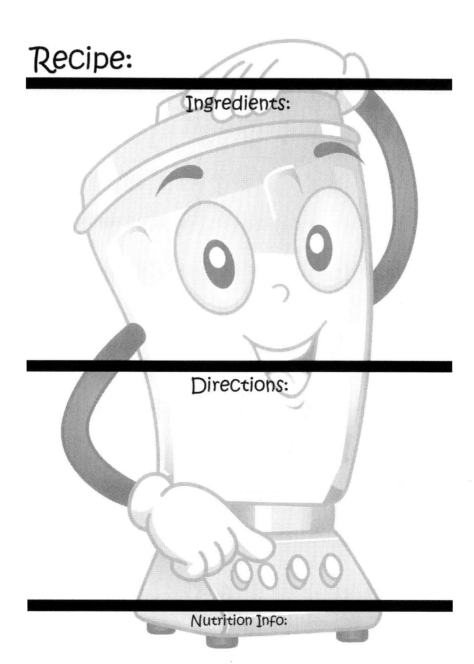

Ingredients:

Directions:

Nutrition Info:

Recipe:

Ingredients:

Directions:

Nutrition Info:

Recipe:

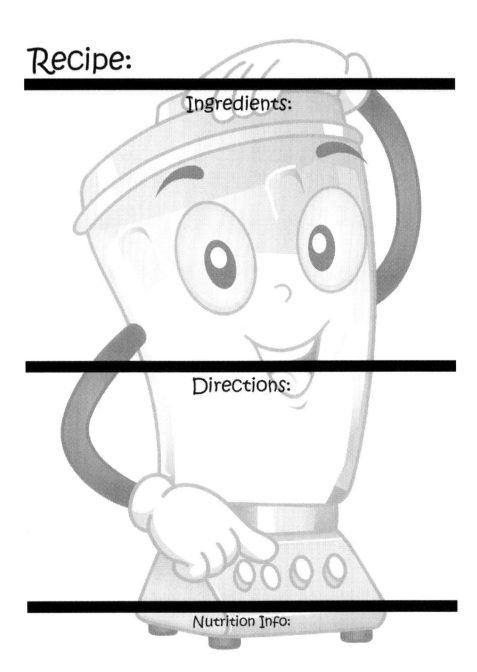

Ingredients:

Directions:

Nutrition Info:

Recipe:

Ingredients:

Directions:

Nutrition Info:

Recipe:

Ingredients:

Directions:

Nutrition Info:

Recipe:

Ingredients:

Directions:

Nutrition Info:

Recipe:

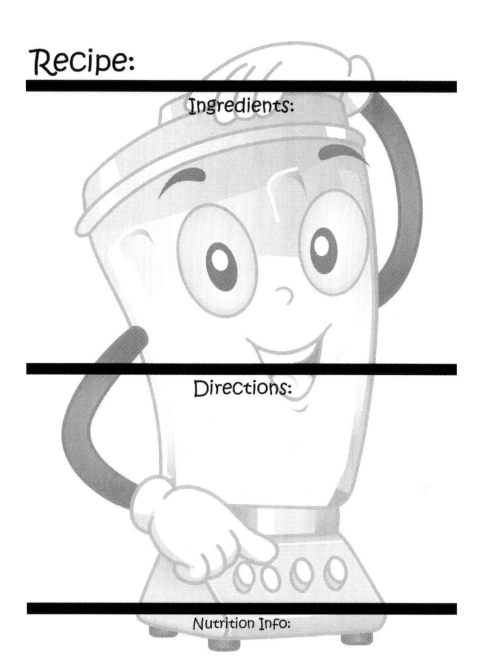

Ingredients:

Directions:

Nutrition Info:

Recipe:

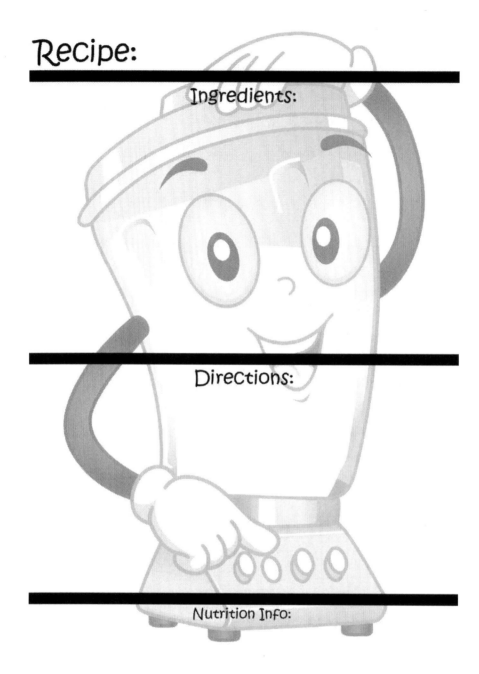

Ingredients:

Directions:

Nutrition Info:

Recipe:

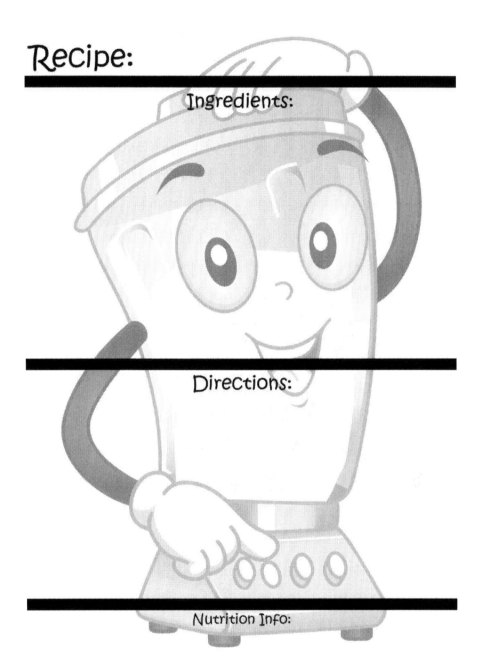

Ingredients:

Directions:

Nutrition Info:

Recipe:

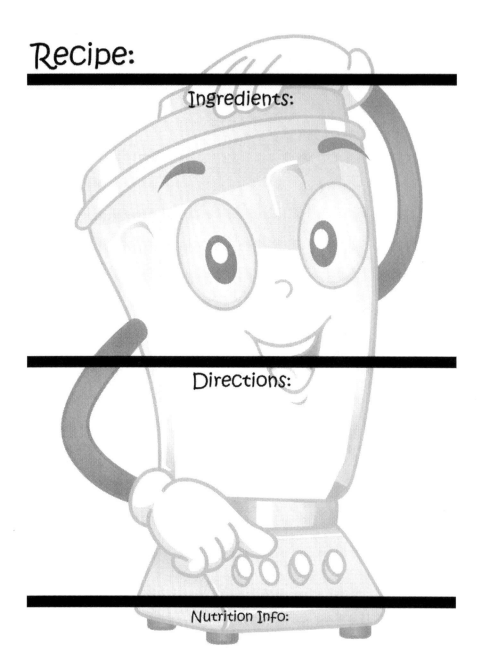

Ingredients:

Directions:

Nutrition Info:

Recipe:

Ingredients:

Directions:

Nutrition Info:

Recipe:

Ingredients:

Directions:

Nutrition Info:

Recipe:

Ingredients:

Directions:

Nutrition Info:

Recipe:

Ingredients:

Directions:

Nutrition Info:

Recipe:

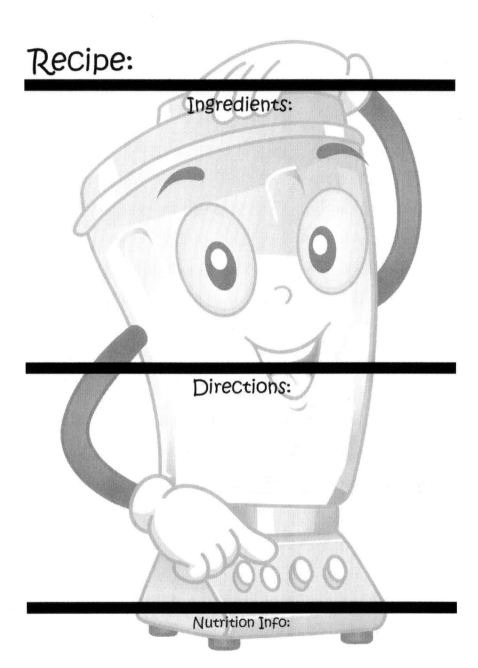

Ingredients:

Directions:

Nutrition Info:

Recipe:

Ingredients:

Directions:

Nutrition Info:

Recipe:

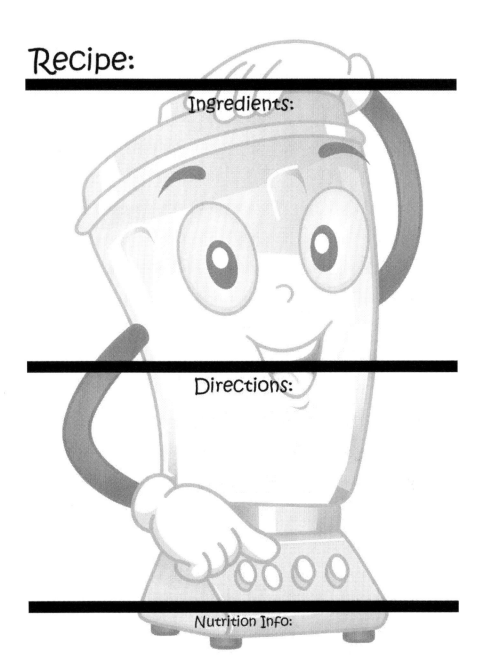

Ingredients:

Directions:

Nutrition Info:

Recipe:

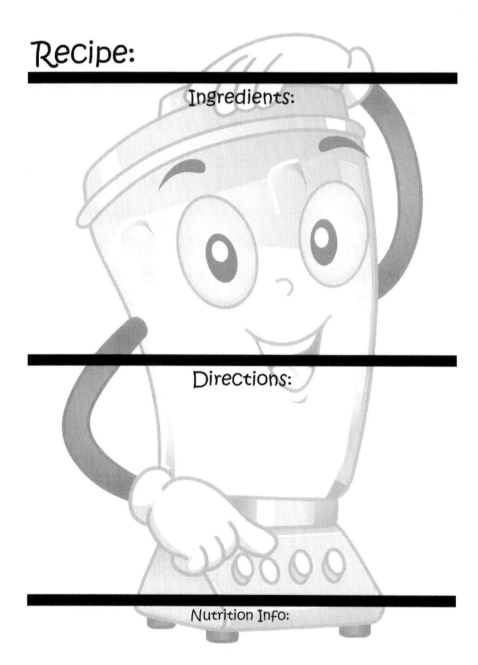

Ingredients:

Directions:

Nutrition Info:

Recipe:

Ingredients:

Directions:

Nutrition Info:

Recipe:

Ingredients:

Directions:

Nutrition Info:

Recipe:

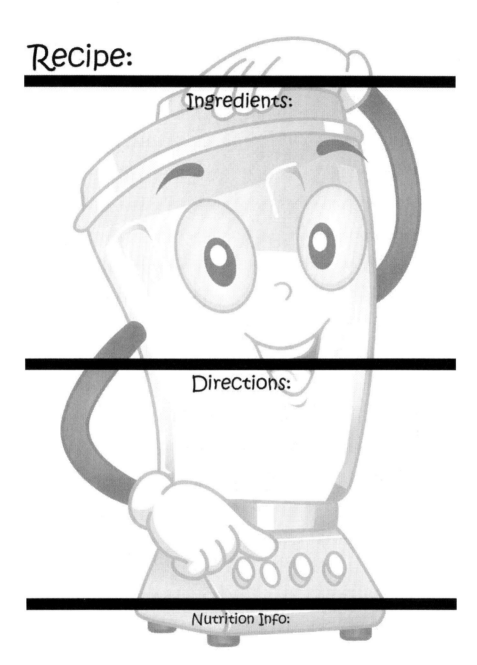

Ingredients:

Directions:

Nutrition Info:

Recipe:

Ingredients:

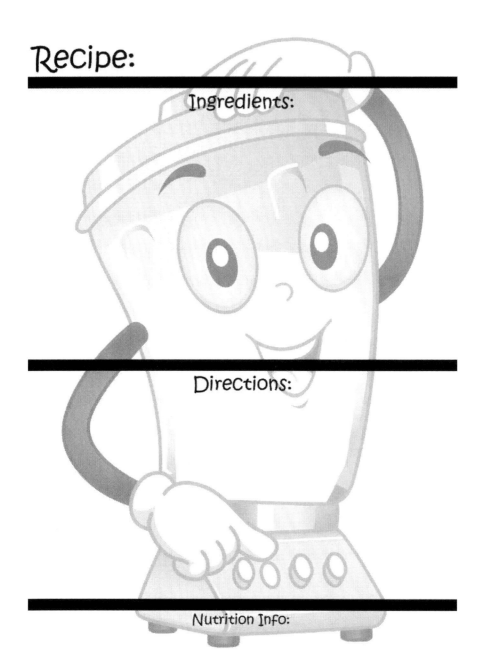

Directions:

Nutrition Info:

Recipe:

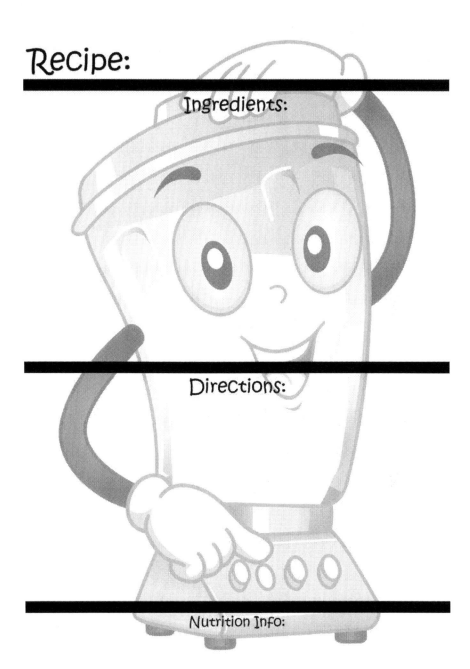

Ingredients:

Directions:

Nutrition Info:

Recipe:

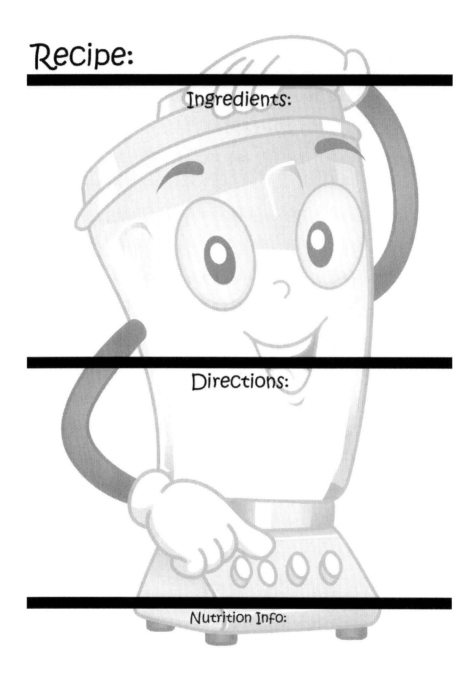

Ingredients:

Directions:

Nutrition Info:

Recipe:

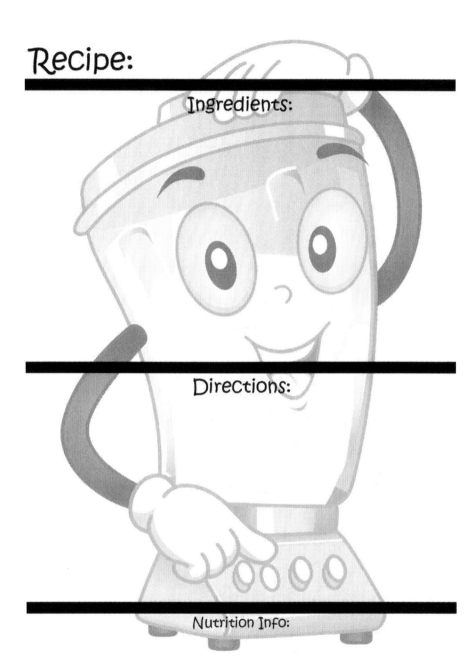

Ingredients:

Directions:

Nutrition Info:

Recipe:

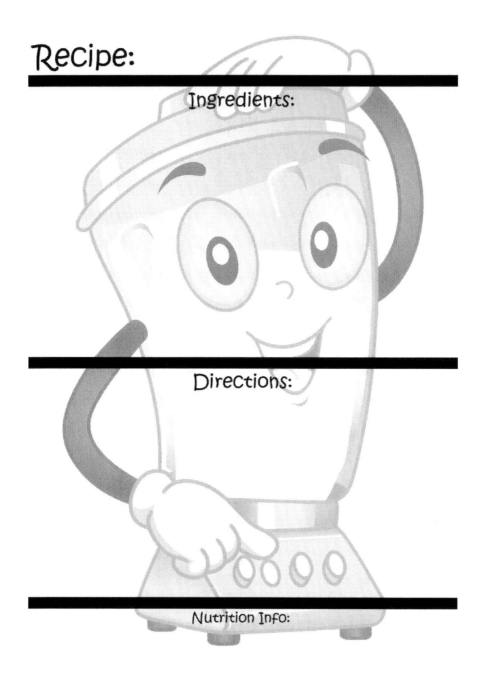

Ingredients:

Directions:

Nutrition Info:

Recipe:

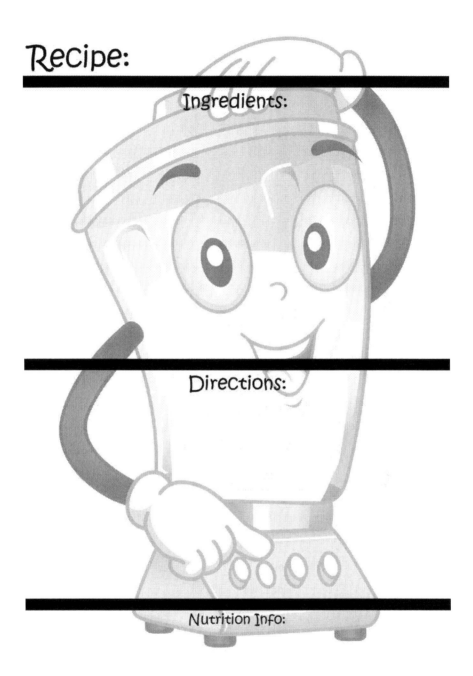

Ingredients:

Directions:

Nutrition Info:

Recipe:

Ingredients:

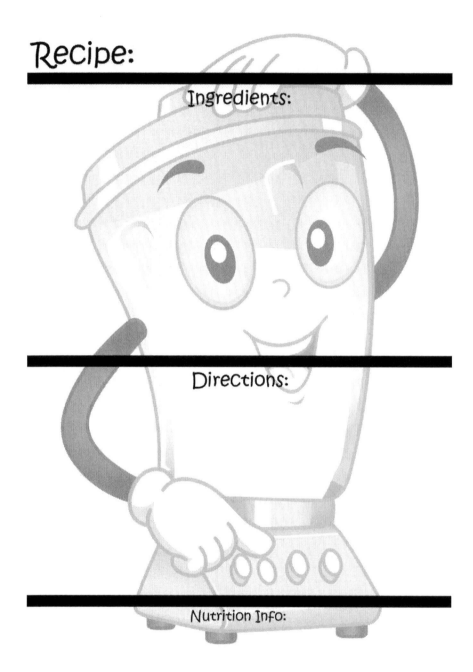

Directions:

Nutrition Info:

Recipe:

Ingredients:

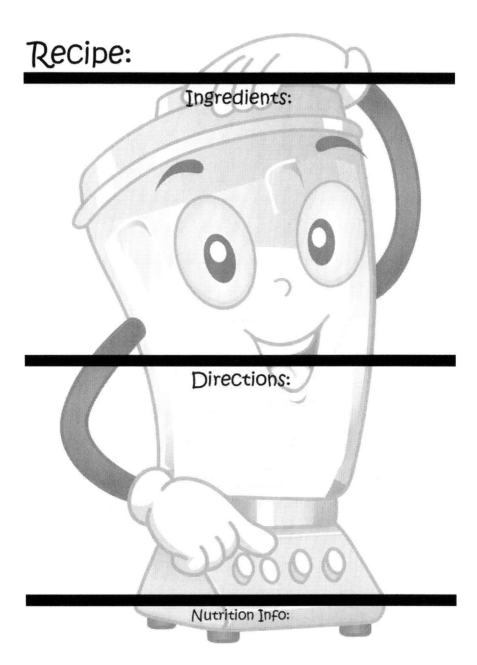

Directions:

Nutrition Info:

Recipe:

Ingredients:

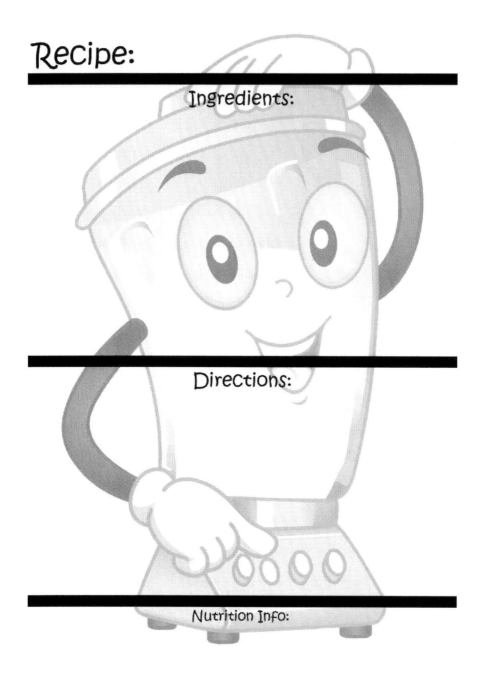

Directions:

Nutrition Info:

Recipe:

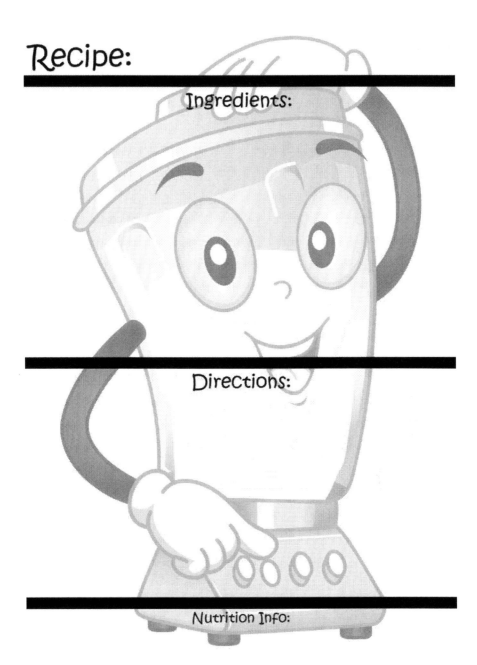

Ingredients:

Directions:

Nutrition Info:

Recipe:

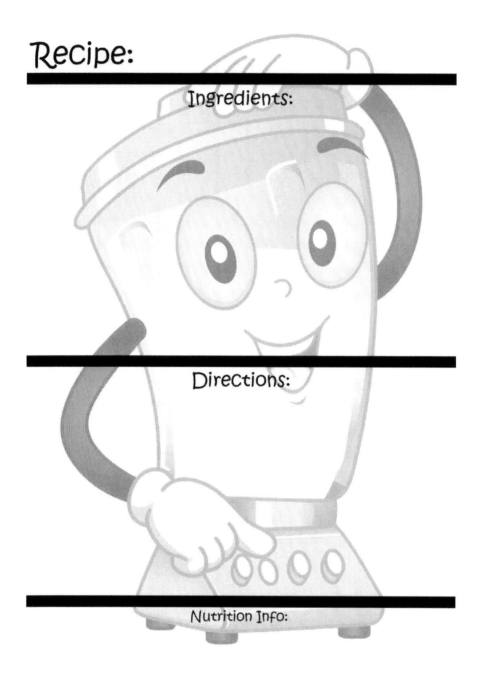

Ingredients:

Directions:

Nutrition Info:

Recipe:

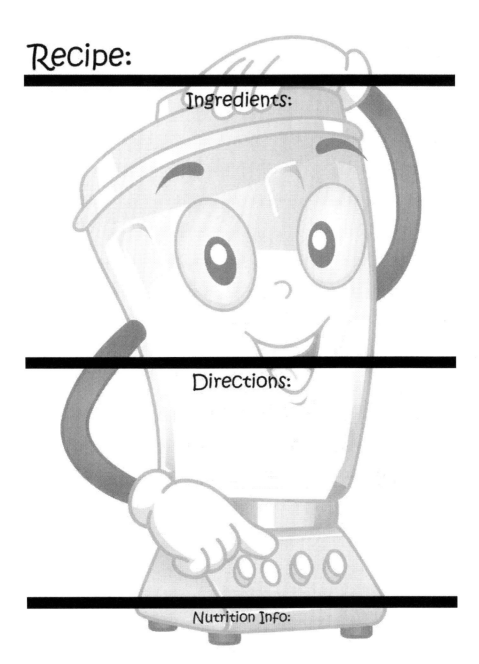

Ingredients:

Directions:

Nutrition Info:

Recipe:

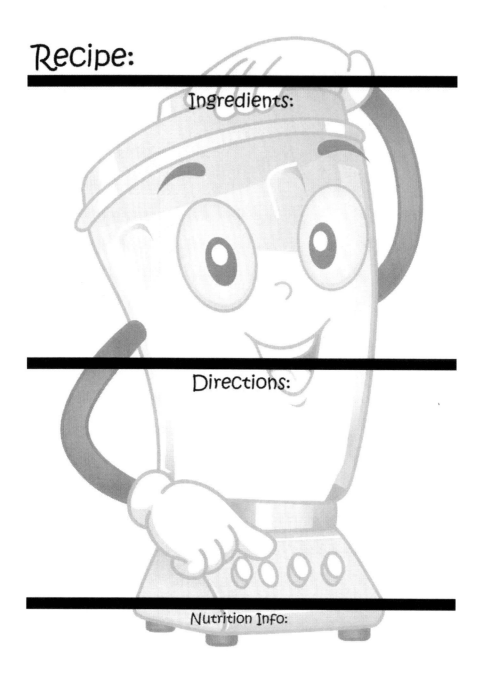

Ingredients:

Directions:

Nutrition Info:

Recipe:

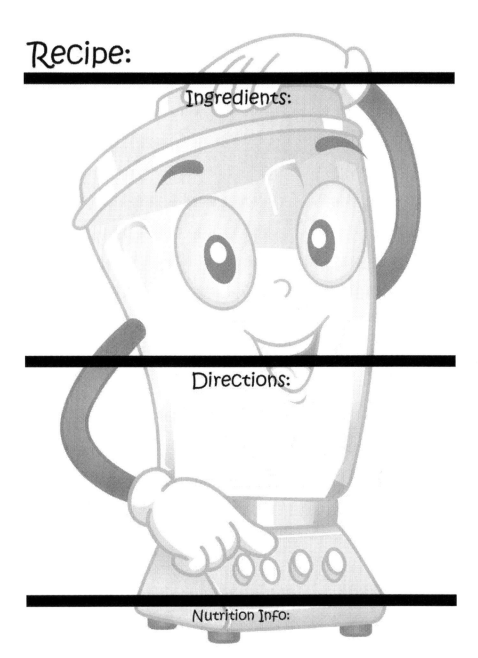

Ingredients:

Directions:

Nutrition Info:

Recipe:

Ingredients:

Directions:

Nutrition Info:

Recipe:

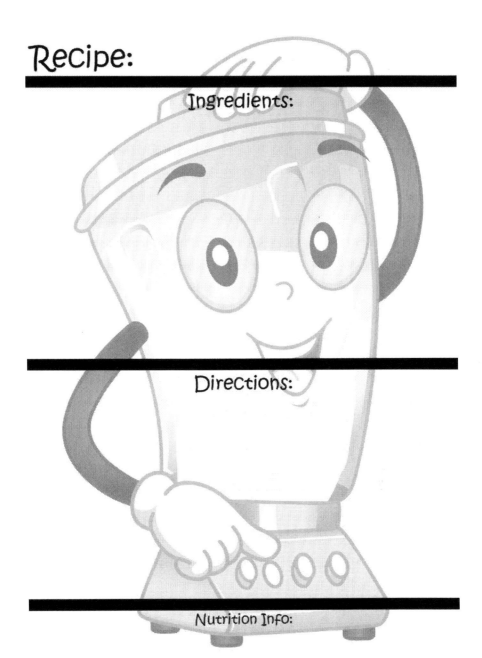

Ingredients:

Directions:

Nutrition Info:

Recipe:

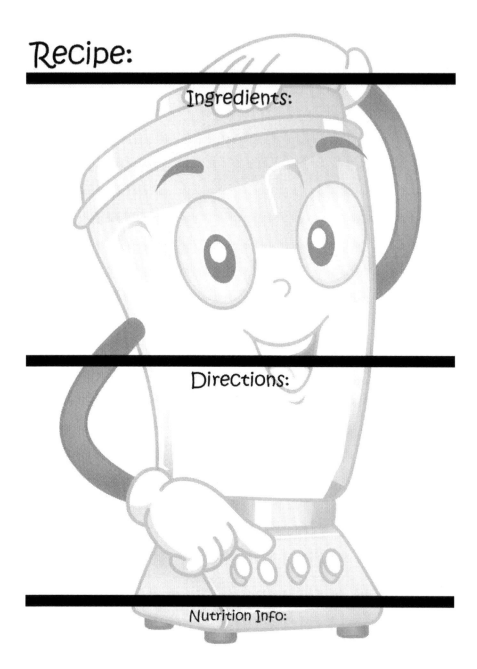

Ingredients:

Directions:

Nutrition Info:

Recipe:

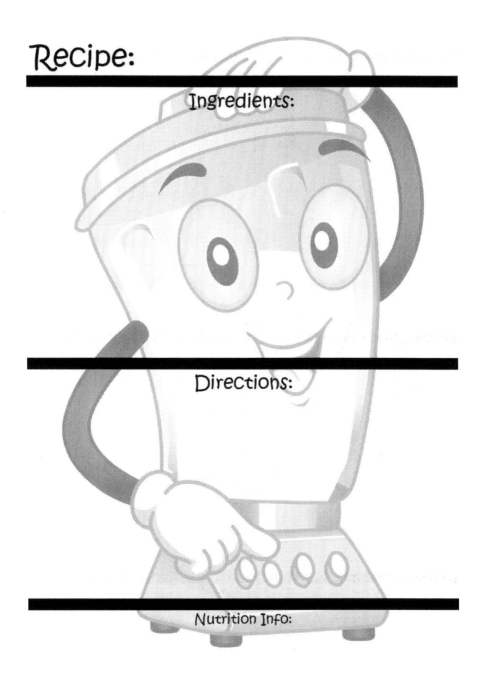

Ingredients:

Directions:

Nutrition Info:

Recipe:

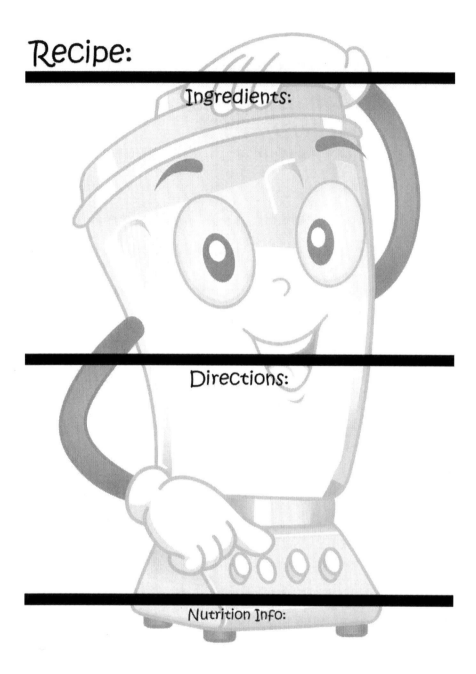

Ingredients:

Directions:

Nutrition Info:

Recipe:

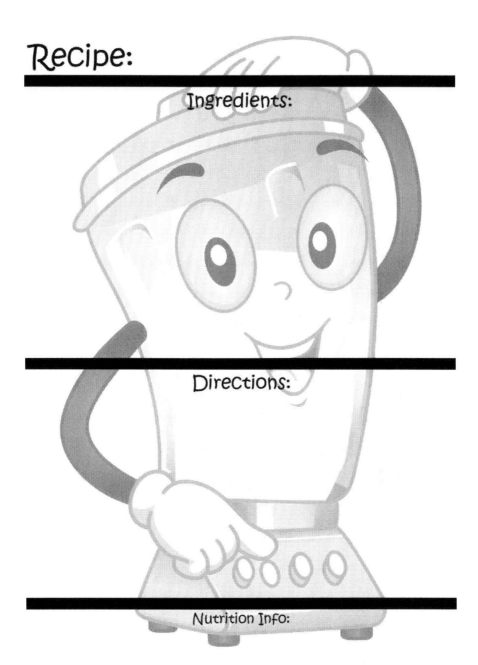

Ingredients:

Directions:

Nutrition Info:

Recipe:

Ingredients:

Directions:

Nutrition Info:

Recipe:

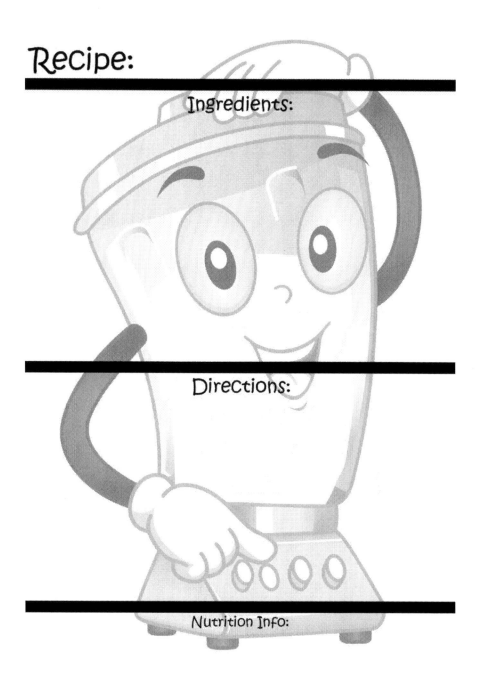

Ingredients:

Directions:

Nutrition Info:

Recipe:

Ingredients:

Directions:

Nutrition Info:

Recipe:

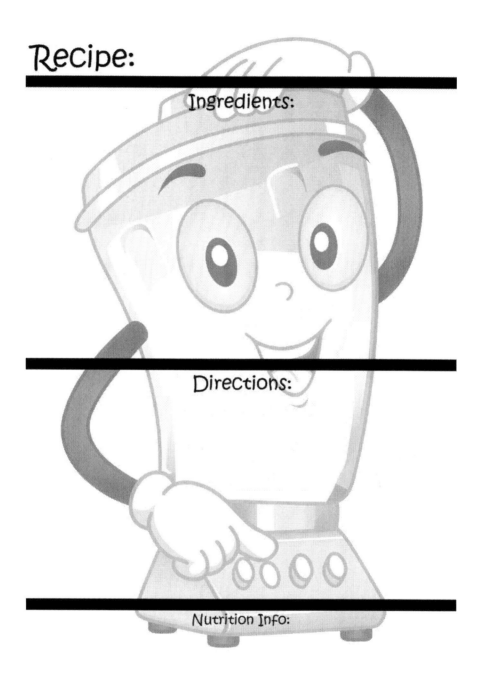

Ingredients:

Directions:

Nutrition Info:

Recipe:

Ingredients:

Directions:

Nutrition Info:

Made in the USA
Middletown, DE
03 November 2022

13991352R00060